DRUM PLAY-ALONG

POP SONGS FOR KIDS

AUDIO ACCESS INCLUDED

CONTENTS

2 Bad Day DANIEL POWTER

6 Can't Stop the Feeling JUSTIN TIMBERLAKE

12 Castle on the Hill ED SHEERAN

22 Counting Stars ONEREPUBLIC

17 Love Story TAYLOR SWIFT

28 Party in the U.S.A. MILEY CYRUS

36 Sugar MAROON 5

32 What Makes You Beautiful ONE DIRECTION

PLAYBACK+
Speed • Pitch • Balance • Loop

To access audio visit:
www.halleonard.com/mylibrary
Enter Code
5887-1254-8122-2558

ISBN 978-1-5400-5916-1

Visit Hal Leonard Online at
www.halleonard.com

Contact Us:
Hal Leonard
7777 West Bluemound Road
Milwaukee, WI 53213
Email: info@halleonard.com

In Europe contact:
Hal Leonard Europe Limited
42 Wigmore Street
Marylebone, London, W1U 2RN
Email: info@halleonardeurope.com

In Australia contact:
Hal Leonard Australia Pty. Ltd.
4 Lentara Court
Cheltenham, Victoria, 3192 Australia
Email: info@halleonard.com.au

Bad Day

Words and Music by Daniel Powter

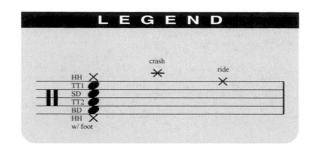

Intro

Verse

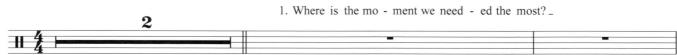

1. Where is the mo - ment we need - ed the most?

You kick up the leaves _ and the mag - ic is lost. __

They tell me your blue _ skies fade _ to grey. __ They tell me your pas - sion's gone _ a - way,,

_ and I don't need _ no car - ryin' on. __

Verse

2. You stand in the line _ just to hit a new low. __

You're fak - in' the smile _ with the cof-fee to go. __

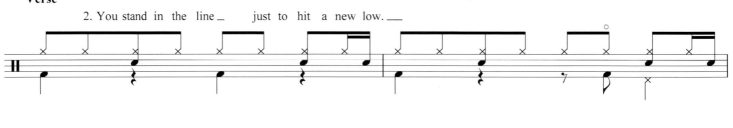

They tell me your life's been way off line. You've fall-en to piec - es ev - 'ry time,

and I don't need no car - ryin' on be-cause you had a bad

%̸ Chorus

day. You're tak-in' one down. You sing a sad song just to turn it a - round. You say you don't

know. You tell me don't lie. You work at a smile, and you go for a ride. You had a bad

To Coda ⊕

day. The cam-'ra don't lie. You're com-in' back down, and you real-ly don't mind. You had a bad

day. You had a bad day.

Verse

3. Well, you need a blue sky hol - i - day. The point is they laugh at what you say,

and I don't need no car - ryin' on. _____ You had a bad

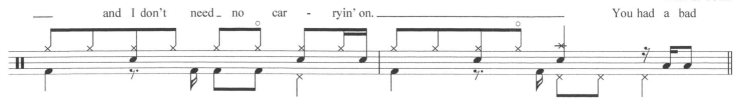

Coda

day. ___ Ooh, _____ on a hol - i - day. ___

Bridge

Some - times the sys - tem goes __ on the blink __ and the whole thing, it turns out wrong. __ You

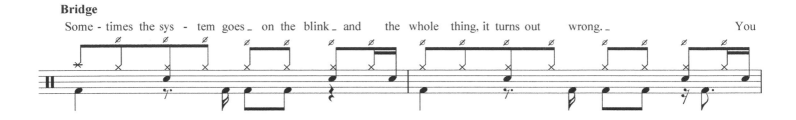

might not make it back, __ and you know __ that you could be well. Oh, that's strong, __ and I'm not wrong, __

_____ yeah. _____

Verse

4. So where is the pas - sion when you need it the most? __ Oh, ___ you and I. __

You kick up the leaves, __ and the mag - ic is lost __ 'cause you had a bad

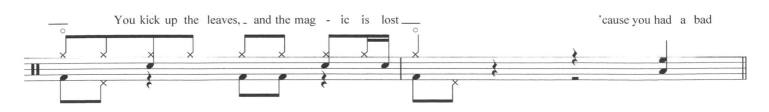

Chorus

day. You're tak-in' one down. You sing a sad song just to turn it a - round. _ You say you don't

know. You tell me don't lie. You work at a smile, _ and you go for a ride. _ You had a bad

day. You've seen what you like. _ And how does it feel _ one more time? _ You had a bad

Outro

day. _ You had a bad day.

Begin fade

Fade out

5

Can't Stop the Feeling

from TROLLS

Words and Music by Justin Timberlake, Max Martin and Shellback

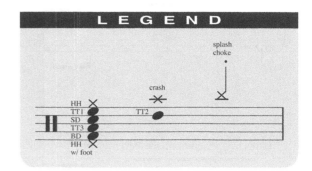

Intro
Moderately ♩ = 113

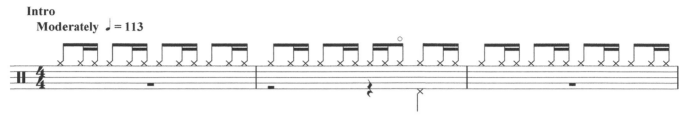

Verse

1. I've got this feel-in' in - side my bones. It goes e -

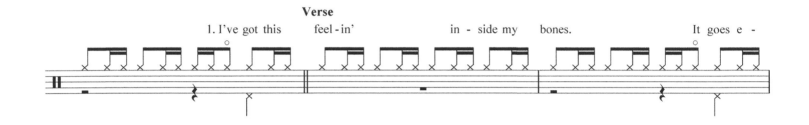

lec - tric, wav - y when I turn it on. All through my

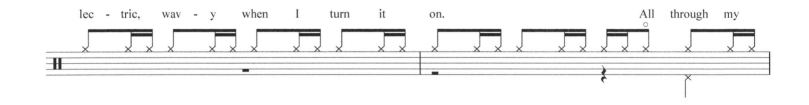

cit - y, all through my home, _____ we're fly - in'

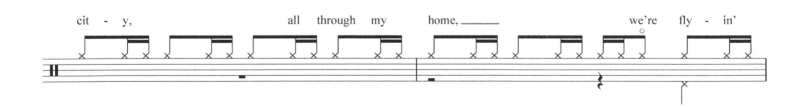

up, no ceil - in' when we in our zone. I got that

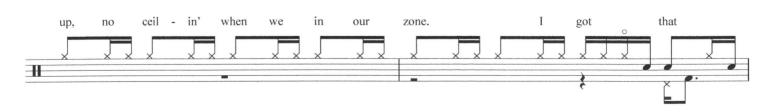

Pre-Chorus

2nd time, substitute Fill 1

Fill 1

Chorus

To Coda ⊕

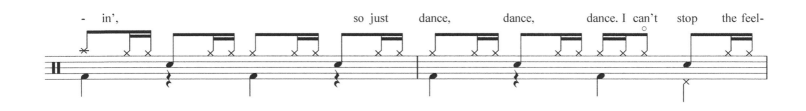

Verse

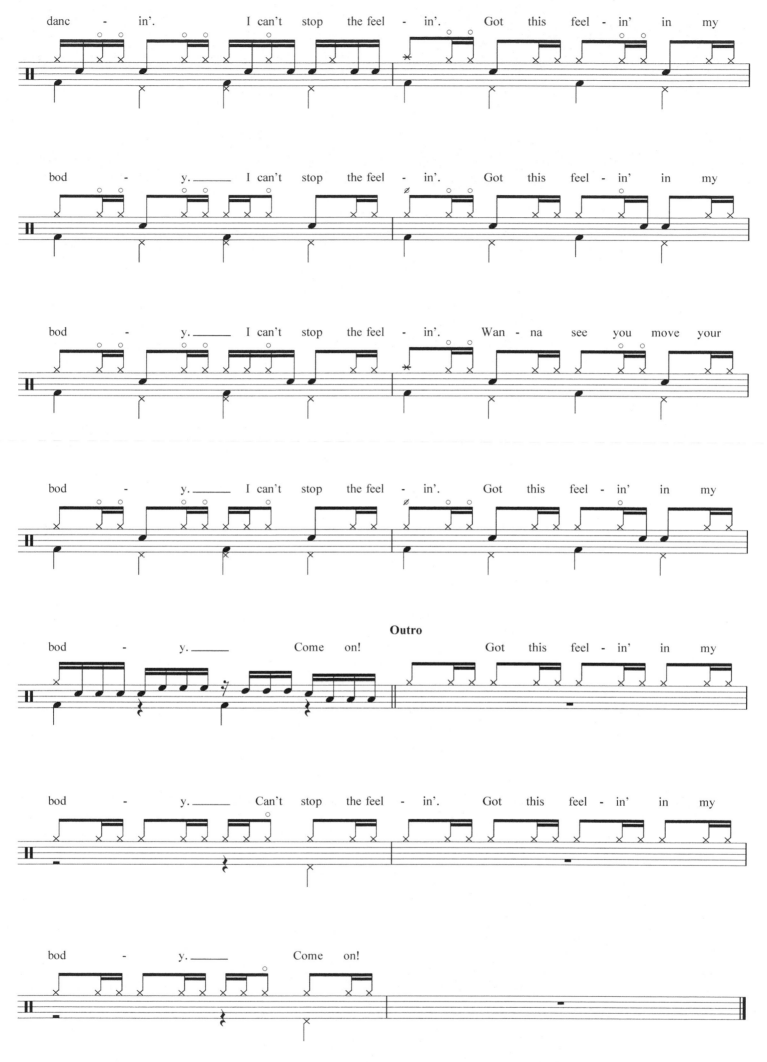

Castle on the Hill

Words and Music by Ed Sheeran and Benjamin Levin

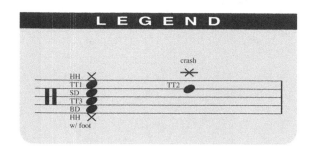

Intro
Moderately fast ♩ = 135

Verse

1. When I was six years old I broke my leg.
2. *See additional lyrics*

I was run - ning from my broth - er and his

friends, and tast - ed the sweet

per - fume of the moun - tain grass I rolled down.

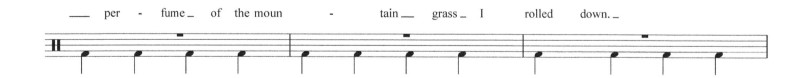

I was young - er then. Take me back to when

I miss _ the way _____ you make me _ feel,

and it's _ real. And we watched _ the sun _____ set _ o -

- ver _ the cas - tle on _ the hill. Hoo, _____ hoo, _____

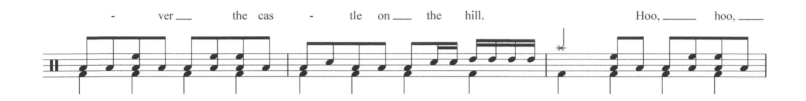

_____ o - ver _ the cas - tle on _ the hill.

Hoo, _____ hoo, _____ o - ver _ the cas -

Outro

- tle on _ the hill.

Additional Lyrics

2. Fifteen years old and smoking hand-rolled cigarettes,
Runnin' from the law through the backfields and gettin' drunk with my friends.
Had my first kiss on a Friday night; I don't reckon that I did it right.
But I was younger then, take me back to when

Pre-Chorus We found weekend jobs and when we got paid
We'd buy cheap spirits and drink them straight.
Me and my friends have not thrown up in so long, oh, how we've grown.
But I can't wait to go home.

Love Story

Words and Music by Taylor Swift

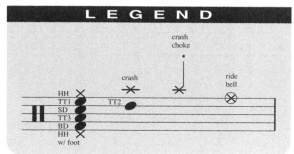

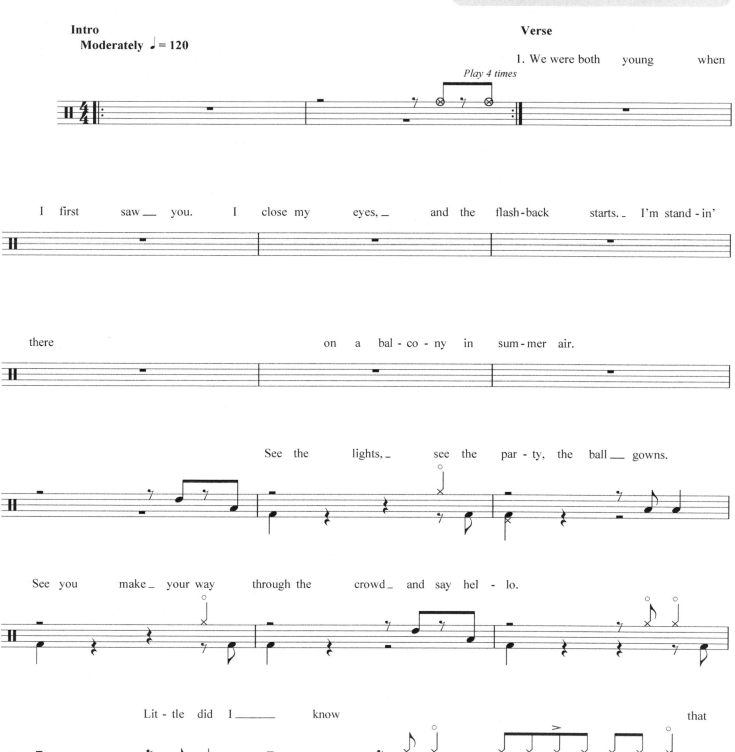

Chorus

"Ro - me - o, save __ me. I've been feel - in' so a - lone." I keep wait - ing

for you, but you nev - er come. Is this in my head? I don't know what to think. He __

knelt to the ground and pulled out a ring and said, **Chorus** "Mar - ry me, Ju - li - et. You'll

nev - er have to be a - lone. I love you, __ and that's all I real - ly know. I

talked to your dad, go pick out a white dress. It's a love sto - ry. __

Outro

Ba - by, just say __ yes." __ Oh, oh, oh. __

__ Oh, oh, oh, __ oh. 'Cause

we were both young when I first saw __ you. __

21

Counting Stars

Words and Music by Ryan Tedder

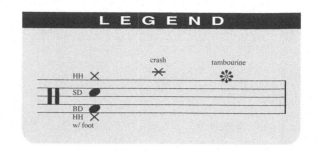

Intro
Moderately ♩ = 108

Late - ly, I been, I been los - in' sleep _____ dream - in' a - bout _ the things that

we could be. But ba - by, I been, I been pray - in' hard. _

Said no more count - in' dol - lars, we'll be count - in' stars. _____ Yeah, we'll be count - in'

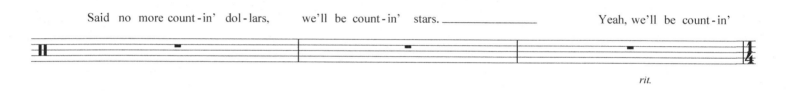

rit.

Faster ♩ = 122

stars.

Verse
1. I see this life like a swing - in' vine, _ swing my heart a - cross the line. _

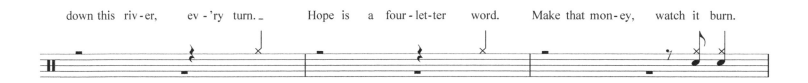

down this riv-er, ev-'ry turn.___ Hope is a four-let-ter word. Make that mon-ey, watch it burn.

Old, but I'm not that old. Young, but I'm not that bold. And I don't think the world is sold

Pre-Chorus

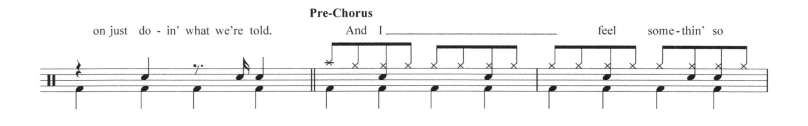

on just do-in' what we're told. And I _____ feel some-thin' so

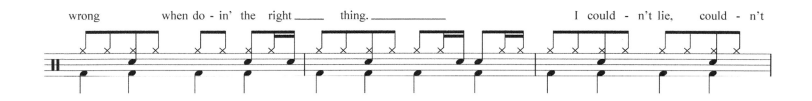

wrong when do-in' the right ____ thing. _____ I could-n't lie, could-n't

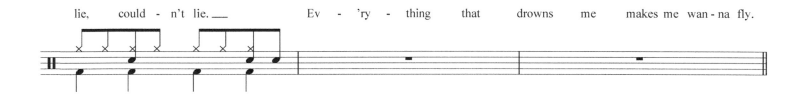

lie, could-n't lie. __ Ev-'ry-thing that drowns me makes me wan-na fly.

𝄋 Chorus

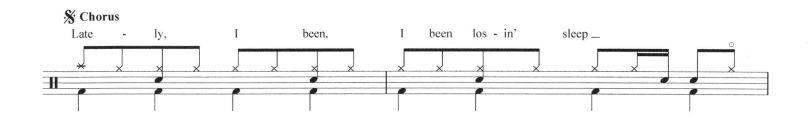

Late - ly, I been, I been los-in' sleep __

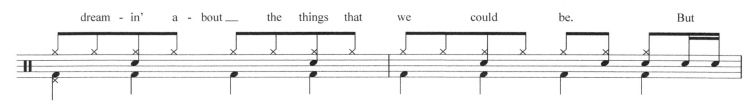

dream-in' a-bout__ the things that we could be. But

To Coda ⊕

Bridge

Party in the U.S.A.

Words and Music by Jessica Cornish, Lukasz Gottwald and Claude Kelly

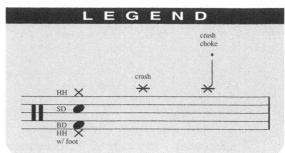

Intro
Moderate Pop ♩ = 96

Verse

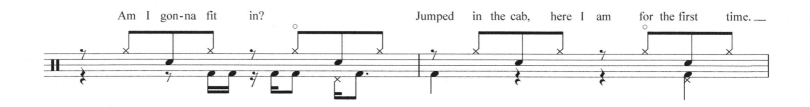

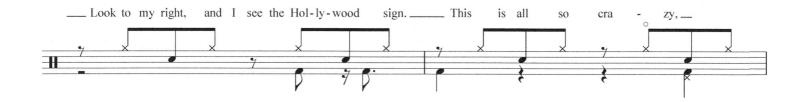

D.S. al Coda

✛ **Coda**

Bridge

What Makes You Beautiful

Words and Music by Savan Kotecha, Rami Yacoub and Carl Falk

shy   and turn a - way   when I look in - to your   eye - eye - eyes.

Coda

Interlude

Na,   na, na, na,   na, na, na,   na, __ na.   Na,   na, na, na,   na, na.

Na,   na, na, na,   na, na, na,   na, __ na.

Na,   na, na, na,   na, na.   **Bridge**
                                        Ba - by, you   light   up __ my world   like __ no -

bod - y else. __ The way that   you   flip __ your hair   gets __ me   o - ver - whelmed. __ But when you

smile   at __ the ground   it __ ain't hard   to tell __ you don't __ know   - oh - oh,

Outro-Chorus
you don't know you're beau - ti - ful.
          Ba - by, you   light up __ my world   like __ no - bod - y else. __ The way that

you flip_ your hair gets_ me o - ver - whelmed._ But when you smile at_ the ground, it_ ain't

hard to tell__ you don't_ know - oh - oh, you don't know you're beau - ti - ful.

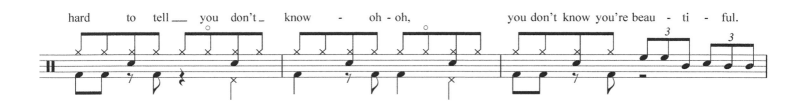

If on - ly you saw_ what I can see,__ you'll un - der - stand why_ I want you_ so

des - p'rate - ly.___ Right now I'm look - in'_ at you, and_ I can't be - lieve_ you don't_

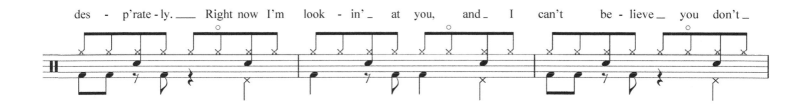

know - oh - oh, you don't know you're beau - ti - ful. Oh - oh - oh,

you don't know you're beau - ti - ful. Oh - oh - oh, that's what makes you beau - ti - ful.

Sugar

Words and Music by Adam Levine, Henry Walter, Joshua Coleman,
Lukasz Gottwald, Jacob Kasher Hindlin and Mike Posner

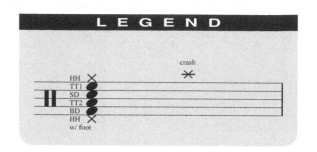

Intro
Moderately ♩ = 120

Verse

1. I'm hurt-in', ba-by; I'm bro-ken down.

I need your lov-in', lov-in'; I need it now. When I'm with-out you,

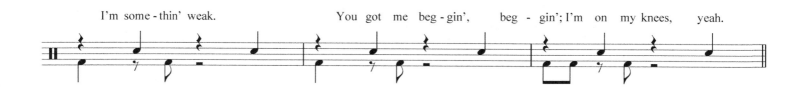

I'm some-thin' weak. You got me beg-gin', beg-gin'; I'm on my knees, yeah.

Pre-Chorus

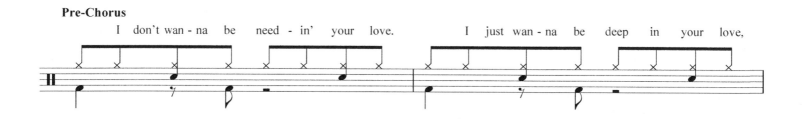

I don't wan-na be need-in' your love. I just wan-na be deep in your love,

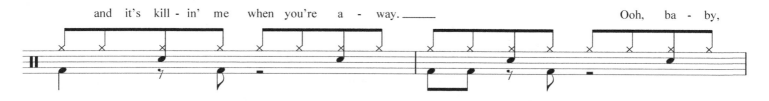

and it's kill-in' me when you're a-way. Ooh, ba-by,

Verse

2. My bro - ken piec - es, you pick them up. Don't leave me hang - in', hang-

in'; come give me some. When I'm with - out you, I'm so in - se - cure.

You are the one thing, one thing I'm liv - in' for.

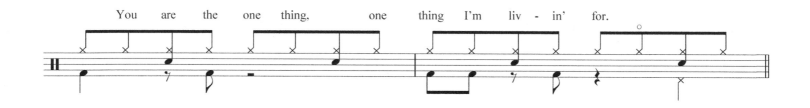

Pre-Chorus

I don't wan - na be need - in' your love. I just wan - na be deep in your love,

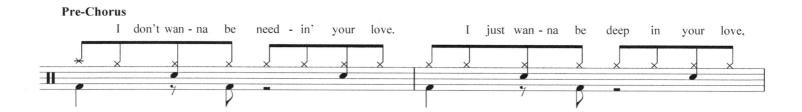

and it's kill - in' me when you're a - way. _____ Ooh, ba - by,

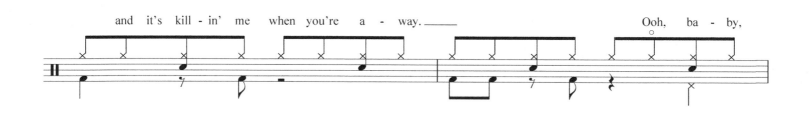

'cause I real - ly don't care where you are. I just wan - na be there where you are,

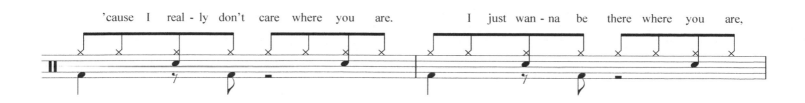

D.S. al Coda

Coda

and I got-ta get one lit-tle taste. ___ You're sug -

Bridge

I want that red vel-vet; I want that sug-ar sweet. Don't let no-bod-y touch it

un-less that some-bod-y's me. I got-ta be a man; there ain't no oth-er way.

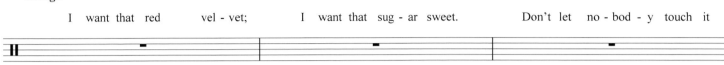

'Cause, girl, you're hot-ter than a south-ern Cal-i-for-nia day. ___

___ I don't wan-na play no games; I don't got-ta be a-fraid.

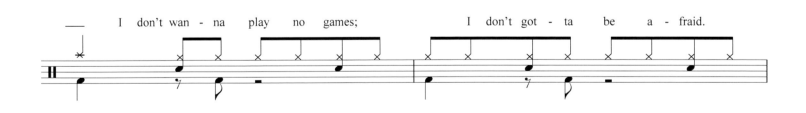

Don't give me all that shy sh*t, no make-up on. That's my sug -

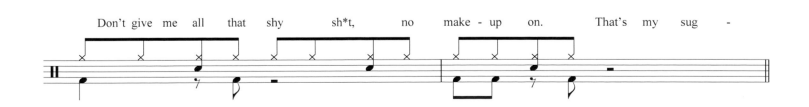

Chorus